THE BIG MLM LIE

Why Multi Level Marketing Sucks

Lisa-Marie Fox

Copyright © 2023 Lisa-Marie Fox

All rights reserved

The characters and events portrayed in this book are fictitious. Any similarity to real persons, living or dead, is coincidental and not intended by the author.

No part of this book may be reproduced, or stored in a retrieval system, or transmitted in any form or by any means, electronic, mechanical, photocopying, recording, or otherwise, without express written permission of the publisher.

CONTENTS

Title Page
Copyright
INTRODUCTION 1
THE DISMAL STATISTICS 7
SO, WHAT'S THE REAL PROBLEM WITH MLM? 9
THE DIFFERENCE BETWEEN MLM AND PYRAMID SCHEMES 10
THE PSYCHOLOGY OF SALES 13
HOW TO ANNOY PEOPLE AND ALIENATE THEM 23
ARE THERE ANY REAL BENEFITS TO MLM? 31
HOW TO AVOID THE HIGH-PRESSURE MLM SALES PITCH 36
LEAVING AN MLM 40
EVALUATING AN MLM OPPORTUNITY 44
THE HIDDEN COSTS OF MLM 46
CONCLUSION 50
MLM GLOSSARY 51

INTRODUCTION

This book could save you a fortune! I know that's a big claim, but please stick with me for a few minutes, and I'll explain how. If you or someone you care about has joined or is considering joining a multi-level marketing (MLM) company, I would appreciate a few minutes of your time. I'll reveal some of the darker secrets of MLM and cut through the hype. Once you have finished reading, you can make a balanced decision about whether you want to get involved.

With the cost-of-living crisis starting to bite, the idea of starting your own business without a significant outlay can seem very tempting. Many of us are seeking an additional income to help cover the rising costs of everyday life. In the last twelve months alone, heating and energy costs have skyrocketed, food prices have increased, and economic uncertainty appears to be set to continue. Turning to MLM or direct selling opportunities can be a tempting way to earn a little extra money.

MLM recruitment surges when the economy is struggling. When things look bleak, it's natural to turn to anything that provides a glimmer of hope. Around 1 in 13 adults in the USA have participated in multi-level marketing activity at some point in their lives, and that number is set to increase.

We are conditioned to believe that hard work and effort will help us to rise to the top. Money is the reward for dedication, commitment, and self-belief. We have a natural desire to be successful, and MLM promises that anyone can succeed if they are willing to put in the effort.

The explosion in popularity of social media means that multi-level marketing opportunities are never far away. "Boss babes" and "Huns" are falling over themselves to spam you with sales pitches for the "opportunity of a lifetime", often using less-than-ethical tactics to try to convince you to join the next big thing. Social media pages are packed with inspirational quotes and mantras. You get invited to groups you never wanted to join. Your private messages are filled with thinly disguised sales pitches? Sound familiar?

For many people, the thought of being self-employed and working the hours they want is a dream come true. Imagine not being confined to an office or factory and being able to choose your own workdays and hours. Envision having a passive income generated by others you bring into the opportunity. MLM is all about friends helping friends to make money and be happy. A simplified, whitewashed dream that we want to believe.

Financial freedom, the chance to make money doing something you love, and a business that fits around your family are just some of the hooks that MLM distributors use to draw you in. Then there are the perks, the potential to earn luxury cars, exotic holidays and the lifestyle of your dreams.

You are led into thinking that you can reach the stars if you want it hard enough. In the MLM world, anything can be achieved by anyone willing to work hard enough. Seize the day! Don't miss out! Believe, and you will achieve! The slick marketing and trendy catchphrases attract thousands of new recruits every year. But is it all based on reality or just fantasy?

The unglamorous truth behind all the glitzy promotions is that MLM is not a stairway to the stars for most people. There is a dark side to MLM and an uncomfortable truth that most people who join MLM companies will not make any or very little money. Some will find themselves considerably out of pocket. The presenters never mention this at the recruitment meetings. This is the other side of MLM, which is kept well hidden amongst the happy, smiling faces of the upline - the truth behind the lie.

I was involved in MLM for well over 20 years. I polished my sales pitch, trained recruits, and even authored articles on MLM for the press. I have worked with various MLM companies, ranging from established names to start-ups. I used to believe in the MLM business model with my whole heart until I began to see and understand the damage it was doing to people's lives.

For every person living the dream, hundreds, if not thousands, more were desperately trying to make the business turn even a tiny profit. It was destroying lives, relationships, and marriages. One couple even cited MLM as the main reason they were considering a divorce.

I'd like you to understand what you are getting into if you consider an MLM opportunity. This book was written to show the other side of MLM, which might not be apparent at first glance.

It is not my intention to single out any MLM company or demonise anyone involved in MLM. There are many good people in the industry (as well as a few not-so-good ones). I don't want to dampen your entrepreneurial spirit or shatter your dreams. I love to encourage free enterprise and want you to succeed. But I don't want you to lose money, hope or self-confidence by getting involved in a system that is almost impossible to beat.

Many defenders in the MLM world believe that anyone who holds an opinion that opposes their ideals is harmful and should be ignored or avoided. Critical thinking is not to be encouraged because that is when the dream starts to unravel.

Some people do make money from MLM -that much is true. But the simple truth is that the vast majority of people do not. Instead, they lose money. And those losses can be significant.

What percentage of people involved in MLM do you think make any money? Fifty per cent? Twenty per cent? Ten per cent? Less? The figure is much less than 1%. Let that sink in for a moment.

Less than 1% of people who get involved in MLMs profit from it. In one study, the loss rate was estimated to be 99.7% [i]

Think about those odds for a second. Will you be among the 0.3% who make it? Realistically? Think of a number between 1 and 333. I chose 243. Did you get it right? If you did, you might have a chance to make a profit. However, if you didn't get it right and chose a different number, you will lose money. Realistically, that's how small the odds are.

Those odds of 1 in 333 don't even relate to making a full-time living from MLM. The odds of achieving a superstar lifestyle from an MLM company are minuscule. Yes, some people achieve it. Some people win the lottery. It's not impossible, but it isn't likely either.

One of the darkest secrets surrounding MLM is its high failure rate. However, anyone who raises an objection or questions anything about the business model is immediately dismissed. MLM companies have even attempted to sue former distributors who spoke out against their products or business practices. Similarly, authors who have criticised the MLM industry as a whole have also faced lawsuits. Of course, it is natural to want to protect one's business interests, but there are more positive ways to preserve a reputation than threatening to sue dissenting voices.

One of the main criticisms of MLM is that it is difficult to have an open and honest conversation about it. Sadly, some companies have become almost cult-like in their attempts to avoid frank discussions of their business practices or products. This secrecy and reluctance to address issues raised have damaged the reputation of the MLM industry, leading many to distrust it inherently. And in some cases, rightly so.

Personal relationships, friendships, and even families have been caught in the crossfire, with lifelong allegiances damaged. A quick internet search reveals countless horror stories of how MLM has affected people on both a social and personal level.

Kays Story
Kay first got involved in MLM when she was a single parent working two jobs and struggling to make ends meet. One day, someone at work

showed Kay a beautiful sparkling bracelet, which Kay admired very much.

Kay's work colleague asked her whether she was interested in making money by selling jewellery just like the bracelet she liked so much. Kay was told that if she sold the jewellery, she would make a commission, and if she recruited people to join the business, she could earn even more.

Kay couldn't afford to splash out any money to get started, but her work colleague offered to pay for Kay's starter kit because she knew Kay would be a great asset to the business.

However, things didn't go as planned. Kay found the jewellery very difficult to sell. She left catalogues with her friends and family, but even though they promised they would look at them, no one wanted to buy anything. Kay still owed her work colleague for the starter kit but found her former friend had become cold towards her. Clearly, she thought Kay wasn't working hard enough or putting enough effort into selling the products or recruiting other people.

Things in the workplace became uncomfortable. Far from being supportive, Kay's sponsor started to criticise everything Kay did. Even when Kay managed to find the money to pay back the loan for the starter kit, things didn't improve. One day, her sponsor came into the office visibly angry. She told Kay that she, too, had failed to meet her quota to stay active in the program, and it was all Kay's fault because she wasn't pulling her weight.

Kay had had enough. It was bad enough that she was being blamed for not being able to sell the jewellery, but now she was being blamed for her sponsor's lack of success too. Kay quit then and there. It wasn't worth the stress and anxiety it was causing her. A couple of months later, her sponsor also quit, but the damage had been done. Their working relationship was never the same again.

If you have heard of the term due diligence, you will know it means thoroughly checking out a business opportunity before deciding whether to invest. And with any business, even one that requires a small investment, such as MLM, it is crucial to understand what you are getting involved in. So, think of this book as a form of due diligence.

This book is quite short and to the point for one reason: it is designed to be read on the fly. No one wants to be wading through a pile of word soup, especially while being pressured into making a decision.

If, after reading this book, you decide you still want to go ahead and sign up – that's OK. You will have considered both sides of the argument and made an informed choice. If, on the other hand, you decide that MLM is not for you, then you can always blame me! Cite this book as the reason you have decided not to get involved. I dare say that I will invoke outrage among a zealous few in the MLM community and will receive some one-star reviews. It's OK; I have thick skin!

On a serious note, I hope this book will stop you from being sold an impossible dream. In these tense economic times when many of us are counting every penny, the prospect of an additional income can be very tempting. MLMs thrive during economic downturns because they recognise that people are more receptive to their message.

If you know anyone else who might find this book helpful, please consider passing it on or recommending it. Buy copies for all your boss-babe buddies!

THE DISMAL STATISTICS

Here are just a few statistics relating to MLM.

It is generally agreed upon, based on multiple sources and studies, that fewer than 1% of individuals who get involved in an MLM will make a profit. UK Justice Norris found in 2008 that out of an MLM participant population of 33,000, *'only about 90 made sufficient incomes to cover the costs of actively building their business.'* **Those** figures translate into a shocking loss rate of 99.7%[ii]

"You'd be hard-pressed to find anyone making over $1.50 an hour- the primary product is opportunity. The strongest, most powerful motivational force today is false hope, Roland Whitsell, Professor of Business[iii]

The results of a 2018 poll conducted among 1,049 MLM sellers revealed that the majority (60%) earned an average of less than $100 in sales over a five-year period, and 20% never made a single sale. The majority of sellers made less than 70 cents per hour. Nearly 32 per cent of those polled acquired credit card debt to finance their involvement in MLM.[iv] [v]

Dr Jon Taylor, in The Case (for and) against Multi-level Marketing, assumes the following drop-out rates, which have been held to be largely accurate.

A minimum of 50% of MLM representatives drop out in the first year.

A minimum of 90% of representatives leave within five years.

By year 10, only those at or near the top have not dropped out—which means at least 95% of representatives have dropped out.[vi]

As we can see, the figures paint a gloomy picture, and if anyone were given this information at the outset, it is doubtful they would want to sign up. Even more concerning is the amount of debt that MLMs create. In one of the cited studies, nearly one-third of recruits used their credit card to finance their business. It is far from the dream of financial freedom that MLM sells.

SO, WHAT'S THE REAL PROBLEM WITH MLM?

MLM, or multi-level marketing to give it its correct title, is a business model which sells products to the public through a network of self-employed distributors. MLM is also called network marketing. Anyone can sign up as a distributor by paying a fee and/or purchasing a starter kit. Distributors are encouraged to recruit others into the business and receive commissions based on their own sales, as well as the sales of those they recruit.

MLM differs from direct selling in that commissions are paid on your own sales and on the sales of those you recruit to the business. These commissions are paid down through several levels, hence the name multi-level. Different MLM companies pay compensation through varying tiers, but there are usually at least three levels – the distributor, their sponsor, and the sponsor's sponsor. A five-tier model was not rare back in the old days of MLM!

There is an obvious problem with the multi-level model: paying compensation to many people means that product prices must be increased to compensate. Massively overpriced products are not uncommon in the world of MLM. Nevertheless, MLM does remain a legitimate form of selling, unlike the model it is often compared with or confused with – the pyramid scheme.

THE DIFFERENCE BETWEEN MLM AND PYRAMID SCHEMES

The key difference between pyramid schemes and MLM schemes is that pyramid schemes pay people to recruit others into the scheme. An MLM business opportunity, on the other hand, must be based on the sales of an actual product.

In a pyramid scheme, only those at the very top will make any money. As people join underneath them in the pyramid, they will receive a portion of the joining costs of the new recruits. Later, investors' money is used to pay those higher up the chain and so on. Eventually, there will be no one left to recruit, and the pyramid will collapse. Pyramid schemes are also known as Ponzi schemes.

Bernie Madoff
Probably the most well-known Ponzi scheme was that run by American businessman and investor Bernie Madoff, who is said to have carried off the largest scam in history. In 2008, Madoff was convicted of running a scheme which falsified trading reports based on investments which did not exist.

The scheme ran for decades and involved billions of dollars. In 2009, Madoff was sentenced to 150 years in prison and ordered to pay $170 billion in restitution. Madoff died on April 14, 2021.

In simple terms, for an MLM to be legal, the compensation scheme must be based on the sales of a legitimate product, and no element of reward without effort should exist. Compensation should be based on sales rather than the number of people recruited. In reality, it is challenging to profit solely from the sales of MLM products. Recruiting others is an essential part of the business's potential.

You might think that MLM is a relatively new concept, but it has been around for nearly 100 years. In the 1940s, a company known as Nutrilite (the California Vitamin Company) introduced a business model based on distributors training other distributors for a share of the profits. Amway purchased Nutrilite in 1972.

In theory, you should be able to join an MLM at any time, even one which has been established for many years and still have the same chance to make money as someone who joined at the very start. This is in direct opposition to a pyramid scheme, where getting in at the beginning is essential for earning any money.

In practice, when an MLM company has been around for some time, the market becomes saturated with its products. When many distributors sell the same product, all competing for a relatively small market share, those who enter the market early, before it becomes saturated, have a better chance of gaining customers than those who come later.

Becoming your own customer and purchasing products to use yourself is one way to "fake" a monthly quota. Officially, it is discouraged, but realistically, many people are doing it because they cannot find any other customers. If you can manage to recruit others who do the same, you have a very precarious business that is only sustainable for as long as your recruits continue to buy their monthly stock. Once people begin to drop out, the business cannot succeed as it has no real customers. You will be out of pocket very quickly.

MLM primarily revolves around selling products, rather than recruiting others. Without genuine customers, your efforts will be in vain.

Choosing the right product is critically important when considering any form of MLM. As with any form of selling, the product you sell is king. If you aren't selling something that people want, then no one will buy it.

Products sold via MLM are often hyped to the point that they rarely live up to the hype. There are exceptions to this rule, but if you charge three times the going rate for a product that people can easily purchase elsewhere, it had better be exceptional. If it's a niche product that's difficult to acquire elsewhere, then you may be on to a winner. However, products aimed at a wider audience need to be special to convince people to buy and keep coming back.

THE PSYCHOLOGY OF SALES

People buy based on psychology. They buy things that will make them feel better, look better or solve a problem. People value scarce items, which is why designed products and limited editions find a market. If the product solves a customer's need, it is an easier sell than something which appeals solely to vanity. Every customer puts a perceived value on a product – if they don't think the product is worth the asking price, they simply won't buy. Of course, some high-pressure sales tactics might FORCE them to buy, but you will never get a repeat customer by using this sort of technique.

Buyers buy feelings. They buy based on how a product will make them feel. In the past, salespeople were taught to sell products based on their features and benefits. These days, we know that customers want to feel like they have made a smart decision. Help to convince a customer that they are making a smart decision in buying your product, and the sale becomes easy.

Part of making a smart decision for a customer means that they feel the purchase is worth the price. This does not necessarily mean that the product must be inexpensive – people are willing to shell out thousands, even millions of dollars, on prestigious products. The luxury sports car market, for example, markets that feeling of excitement, exhilaration, and freedom which your average family car doesn't provide. People are willing to pay the price of the luxury car even though it effectively gets you from A to B in the same way as the average car, albeit a bit faster and in a bit more style.

A sticking point arises when a customer perceives the value of an item to be less than its price. This may be because they have no use for the item, no need for it, or they can obtain a better value elsewhere.

OVER-PRICED PRODUCTS

Many items sold via MLM are simply priced too high for the market. Back in the early days, when I sold diet products in a now-defunct MLM, I delivered a great sales pitch. Customers were ready to buy, but when they found out the price of a month's supply of the product, they immediately baulked. Because the product was literally five times the regular food cost for the week. Even the intense sales pitch, numerous customer testimonials, and the dream of a new slim body could not overcome that massive stumbling block: the price. It wasn't just me who had the problem. Other distributors had it too. The products were simply priced too high for the market. No one was willing to pay the price, and the company went into liquidation very soon after.

As you may have already realised, the more compensation levels an MLM offers, the more the end price must be increased to compensate. The standard retail chain has the manufacturer, the wholesaler/distributor and the end retailer. In MLM, you have the manufacturer, several tiers of distributors and finally, the end customer. This is why some MLM products are twice or even three times the price of comparable products.

With some products, it is very difficult to ascertain their true value. With a personal development product, the price might be hundreds of times the cost of producing it. It is hard to put a price on the perceived value of the knowledge contained within; some MLM companies are not opposed to capitalising on this. Because no one can truly determine a fair price, these items can sell for hundreds or even thousands of dollars.

If you weren't a distributor or a potential distributor of the product you intend to sell, would you honestly buy the product at the price offered? Think as a potential customer might. Could you justify the purchase? Do you need the product? Do you want the product? What benefits does it offer you? How would it make you feel? If you saw the product in a shop, would you stop to look or walk on by?

New distributors often get excited about the business opportunity and don't thoroughly evaluate the products they will be selling. And I can tell you that in almost all of the MLM opportunities I was involved with over the years, the product quality determines how successful the business becomes – and, indeed, how long it lasts

IS THERE LONG-TERM POTENTIAL?

Does the product lend itself to repeat purchases? Is the product a consumable or a one-off purchase? Consumable items are purchased regularly and used up quickly, such as cosmetics, cleaning products, and vitamins. Customers will regularly purchase, hopefully becoming long-term customers. Having a customer base who regularly buys from you is easier than constantly going out and finding new customers.

One-off purchases or infrequent purchases include items which are designed for longer-term use. These include toys, books, adult items, furniture and clothing. While customers may purchase again from the range, they will not generally make regular purchases. This means that you will constantly be on the lookout for new customers.

There is a third "hybrid" type of category – products purchased once, but allow you to earn recurring fees from that purchase. This includes items such as telecom contracts or other types of ongoing commitments. These are generally more suited to affiliate marketing than MLM, and there is some ambiguity as to whether or not a service can be construed as a product.

Overall, consumable items are lower-priced, easier to sell, and lend themselves well to repeat business. '

IS THERE A MINIMUM SALES REQUIREMENT TO EARN COMMISSIONS?

MLM compensation schemes should be based on selling a legitimate product to an end customer. Rewards for recruiting others should be based on their sales to customers. Take a careful look at the compensation scheme and see if there is a minimum sales requirement to stay "active" in the plan – if there is, this should be a big red flag. You might see this clause described as personal sales volume or distributor commitment. If you fail to meet the sales target, you may not receive compensation for your sales. In practice, distributors end up buying products or "stock" to meet the minimum requirement. This is unsustainable and could result in significant financial losses.

In 2019, the Federal Trade Commission sued an MLM company, claiming it was operating as an illegal pyramid scheme. The FTC claimed that the company made misleading claims regarding potential earnings, and distributors had to purchase thousands of dollars' worth of products a year to be eligible to earn all possible forms of compensation. The company agreed to pay $150 million to settle the case

BUY BACK CLAUSES

One of the most common complaints from individuals involved in MLM schemes is that they are left with unsold inventory upon leaving. This is often due to purchasing products to "stay active" in the scheme or be eligible for commissions. Check to see if your agreement includes a buy-back clause that states the company is willing to repurchase any unsold stock. A legitimate company will typically repurchase its products, although certain terms and conditions may apply.

Even if a buy-back policy is in place, most companies will only purchase items in their original, resaleable condition, and sometimes only in their original, unopened packaging. So, if you have opened a product, even if you have never used it, the company may refuse to accept it. They may only agree to buy back the product at a discounted price.

One very popular US-based MLM changed its buy-back policy seemingly overnight, causing outrage amongst distributors. The initial buy-back policy promised 100% buy-back of inventory purchases with free shipping back to the company. There were apparently no terms and conditions that applied to this clause.

As a result of this policy, distributors felt reassured, and some invested thousands of dollars into stock, knowing that if they couldn't sell it, the company was willing to repurchase it.

However, the company later revised its buy-back policy to offer only a 90% refund, which was applicable only to products ordered directly from the company within the past 12 months. The company stipulated that the items must be in their original packaging and in resalable condition. Additionally, distributors were responsible for covering the shipping costs of returning the inventory to the company.

Not surprisingly, this sudden change of policy caused outrage amongst distributors. Some even launched a class action lawsuit against the company. The company claimed that the 100% buy-back offer had only ever been a temporary arrangement and that the company's standard policy had been the 90% buy-back clause. Unfortunately, this whole debacle resulted in numerous unhappy distributors and negative publicity for the popular MLM.

MARKET SATURATION

The longer an MLM company has been around, and the more distributors it has, the greater the chance that any potential customer has already been exposed to their products. That is why distributors who enter the market at the very beginning, when the products are relatively new, will have an easier time marketing the company's products than those who come later. Products that are new to the market have novelty value and a greater chance that customers have not encountered them before.

That is not to say that making money with a well-established opportunity is impossible. There is some merit to the theory that a company with a long history will be trusted more by potential customers than a newly established one. Their products are likely to be well-known and have a good reputation. But if you name any of the big, well-established MLM companies, a potential customer or business opportunity prospect will likely already know someone who sells the product. You then must work harder to convince them to buy from you than from their existing contact.

LOGISTICS

In the past, most MLM distributors primarily made sales to friends and family. They usually delivered the customer's order directly to them in person. With the advent of the internet, social media and online selling, it is now possible to sell your products anywhere in the world. It is essential to factor in any shipping costs when selling to customers who aren't local.

Some MLMs offer free shipping, but this is usually only within a specific geographic area, and customers outside this area may have to pay a hefty shipping fee to get their goods. If you are selling internationally, ensure you are aware of the various taxes and import duties that may apply to the sale. Not only is this a headache, but it can also significantly impact your profits.

Will you need to hold stock to ship to the customer, or will the company ship directly? Some MLMs offer distributors a sales portal where customers can order items directly, which are then shipped to them. This avoids the need to hold stock and removes the hassle of packing and shipping products. The company will also handle any returns; however, a reduction in the compensation program is likely to reflect this convenience.

Consider how you will be making the bulk of your sales. Will they be online, or do you intend to have parties and either sell products directly or take orders? If it is the latter, you will need to invest in demonstration stock and a selection of top-selling products so that you can fulfil orders quickly. This significantly affects how much you will need to invest in your business.

In today's world, people expect to receive goods they order promptly. How long will customers have to wait to receive their orders? Does the company ship directly to them, and how long does it take? If you need to place an order directly with the company and then ship it to customers, is there a minimum sales threshold you must meet before you can place an order? How quickly will the company ship the product to you, and how quickly can you ensure it reaches your customer? Customers who must wait a long time to receive their order are unlikely to want to order from you again.

SUPPLEMENTS AND HEALTH PRODUCTS

This is a popular area for MLM companies to operate in, but you must be very careful when selling these products to avoid making unverified health claims. Consumer law is very clear in this area. Anyone claiming that a product will treat an existing condition, help you lose weight, or improve your health must ensure that they do not fall foul of the regulations or make unsubstantiated claims.

In the United Kingdom, the Advertising Standards Authority have produced a fact sheet which guides MLM sellers who promote health and wellness products.

Quote:

You need to be careful when advertising a food, drink, or food supplement. The Food Rules will apply to any health claims you make. A 'specific health claim' is a claim like 'this supplement helps with your immune system' or 'supplement X contains Y, which speeds up your metabolism'. To make these claims, they need to be authorised on the GB Nutrition and Health Claims (NHC) Register. ("Food, Food Supplements & Health Claims - Advertising Standards Authority") If the claim is not authorised, you can't make it.

"A 'general health claim' is something like 'good for you, 'healthy', 'superfood', etc. A general health claim needs to be accompanied by an authorised specific health claim to be acceptable." ("Food, Food Supplements & Health Claims - Advertising Standards Authority") If you don't accompany a general health claim with a specific authorised health claim, you may be breaching the Code.

Even if the MLM company whose products you sell is based in another country, you must comply with the code if you are marketing to customers in the UK.

In the United States, health claims must be supported by solid evidence. The FTC and the FDA work together to regulate claims made by advertisers of health and wellness products. MLM companies must ensure that all their distributors are aware of and comply with the law.

The FTC states that

"1) Advertising must be truthful and not misleading."

"2) before disseminating an ad, advertisers must have adequate substantiation for all objective product claims" ("Health Products Compliance Guidance | Federal Trade Commission")

In 2020, the FTC sent warning letters to six MLM companies that either made claims about their products' ability to treat or prevent COVID-19 or claimed that people who had recently lost income due to the pandemic could earn money with their opportunity. And in 2022, two companies were effectively banned from advertising or selling dietary supplements based on their unsubstantiated claims that their products treated cardiovascular disease and diabetic neuropathy.

A reputable MLM company will guide their distributors on what they can or can't legally say about the products. An unscrupulous company will allow distributors to make unfounded claims, which could result in both the company and the distributor facing trouble.

CLAIMS OF EARNINGS

The sad reality is that a substantial portion of people involved in MLM opportunities don't make any money and will lose money. A comprehensive study on the money-making potential of MLM companies, published on the FTC website, found that fewer than 1% of recruits actually generate any income. The 99% failure rate is even worse than that of pyramid schemes, which have a failure rate of around 90%.

This lack of making money is not a new situation. Way back in 1980, the attorney general of Wisconsin investigated approximately 20,000 distributors for a major MLM company who lived in the state. The top 1% of distributors' tax returns were analysed to determine if they were indeed generating income from the opportunity. A shocking truth arose. When their tax returns were analysed and the business's expenses were deducted, the average profit for these "top" distributors came in at around minus $900. When the data were analysed further, those who made a significant income from the business were just 1 in 10,000 of the Wisconsin distributors. If you were a gambler, you certainly wouldn't accept those odds.

There is a culture in some MLMs of fake it until you make it. Thus, it is challenging to determine who is truly generating revenue and who isn't. Behind the glitzy marketing events and star-studded product launches, a different story might emerge.

Anne (not her real name) was one of the leading lights in an MLM company in the early 1990s. She was apparently selling thousands of pounds worth of products each month, and the company constantly used her as an example of how much money could be made by selling their products. On the surface, Anne was the absolute picture of success. She drove an expensive car and had a perma-tan from all the holidays and international conferences the company had sent her on.

But in reality, all was not what it seemed. Anne had been so desperate to make it in the business that she had funded her lavish lifestyle on her credit card. She had used up all her savings by investing in the company's products, which she couldn't sell. She had gone so far as to create "fake" customers, so it appeared that she was legitimately selling products. Huge stockpiles of products were stored in Anne's spare bedroom, threatening to spill over into other rooms of the house. Anne was beside herself with worry and fear as her "empire" came crashing down around her.

Unfortunately, there are many Annes in the world of MLM. Whilst it is illegal to make any claim of specific earnings in an MLM scheme, distributors are often lured in with the promise of a dream life or the inference that they can leave their 9-to-5 job and make a full-time living from the opportunity. These implied claims are unethical and, in some cases, downright illegal; nevertheless, they continue to lure people in.

If you fail at MLM, there is often an inference that you didn't work hard enough or believe in the opportunity enough. That is absolute rubbish, whatever your upline will try to convince you. If you are not making money from MLM, it has nothing at all to do with your work ethic, enthusiasm or how much effort you put in. The cold truth is that the system is flawed, not you. MLM can destroy relationships, confidence, self-esteem and bank balances. Many people are deterred from trying to sell for a living after having tried and failed in MLM.

HOW TO ANNOY PEOPLE AND ALIENATE THEM

How often have you had someone you barely know or have spoken to for the past gazillion years suddenly pop into your inbox? You know what the first words out of their mouth after a brief greeting are going to be. You know they will try to sell you something you probably don't want. How does that make you feel?

The explosion in social media popularity has given MLM distributors a new tool – or, in many cases, a means to abuse it. The truth is that most people who are looking for a business opportunity will find it on their own, not via someone who slides into their DM's

Trying to sell to your friends' list on social media feels like an invasion of privacy for most people. You might get one or two "sympathy" sales, but you risk damaging your friendships. People resent feeling like they need to purchase a product they don't want, and they will remember how you made them feel. If you want to annoy people and alienate them, then harass them and annoy them into buying via your personal social media.

Not only that, but irritate them further by posting endless motivational quotes, positive slogans and hints at how well your business is doing and how they are missing out on the opportunity of a lifetime. Repeat this several times a day for weeks on end, and congratulations, you will have alienated just about everyone on your friend's list. Not surprisingly, many people will start to avoid you for fear that you will try to sell them something.

The phenomenon of MLM distributors attempting to make sales on social media has become so prevalent that a term has even emerged to describe them – hunbots!

Noun. hunbot (plural hunbots) (Internet slang, derogatory) **One who uses false endearments in pursuit of online sales or MLM** (multi-level marketing). ("hunbot - Wiktionary")

Trying to sell on social media feels like an invasion of privacy to many people. If you must sell on social media, use a dedicated sales page, not your personal page. Inviting your friends to like or follow that page is fine but refrain from harassing them if they decline. And don't constantly send out invites to get them to like the page, because that's annoying too.

The initial idea behind MLM - friends selling to friends and helping them make money- is noble. After all, we are conditioned to trust our friends and families, and we believe they have our best interests at heart. We are more likely to try a product that is being used and recommended by someone we trust than one sold to us by a complete stranger.

Unfortunately, some people have abused that trust and taken advantage of the good nature of their friends and families just to sell products. This has not only destroyed relationships but has also led to a deep distrust of MLM for many people. Understanding and respecting other people's perspectives is a crucial aspect of running your business. Don't be that annoying person who is always trying to make a quick buck from their loved ones or constantly trying to get them to change their minds and try the products.

If your MLM product is genuinely changing your life, making you more attractive or helping you lose weight, then your friends and family will notice sooner or later. When they comment on how great you look, sharing how the products have changed your life is acceptable, but don't push it. Let them make their own decision about whether to get involved or not.

Remember, you don't have to do MLM in an annoying way. Ethical and successful MLM distributors are those who build relationships, respect the feelings of others, and focus on helping their customers, rather than just making a sale.

CAN YOU ADD VALUE?

The most successful salespeople go the extra mile to add value to their pitch. Thousands of people are selling the same product, so how will you stand out from the crowd?

As a former MLM trainer, I can tell you that this is the area people tend to think about the least when getting involved in any MLM business. When I asked new recruits how they planned to make sales, I would receive answers like, "Oh, the products will sell themselves," or they had a "secret formula" that would be revealed later. In short, most people didn't have a plan.

MLM is truly a cutthroat world. You are competing against many others selling the same product in a potentially saturated market. You must make yourself appear different and add value to your customer's experience.

Social media provides us with more opportunities than ever to reach new customers and expand into new markets. Lever this to your advantage by offering something that your competitors do not have that your customers perceive as valuable. Could you do make-up tutorials, household cleaning demos or offer genuinely helpful hints, tips or advice on a subject relating to your products?

Unless you can be useful and provide people with a genuine reason to buy from you, you will struggle to succeed. Adding value is a robust marketing tool and will help you generate more sales, leads and customers.

IT'S NOT YOU - IT'S THEM

Mary desperately wanted to provide financial security for her family and some of the little luxuries their current budget couldn't stretch to. After seeing an advertisement for a well-known MLM company, she decided to join and began her journey toward success. Or so she thought. After months of effort, Mary had nothing to show for her time but a few measly sales and lots of very angry friends. She had constantly been pushing her products on her friends and family, but they weren't interested. With no one buying and no signs of success, Mary felt like a failure and eventually quit in frustration.

John had been made redundant. Disillusioned and unable to find any work, he saw an advert for "independent distributors" on a job noticeboard. John had some experience in sales; he had once worked as a travelling salesperson for a small company and was good at talking to people and persuading them to buy. He figured that independent marketing and MLM would be an opportunity for him to build an income on his terms.

John eagerly applied for the position, and a few days later, he found himself at a meeting at a plush hotel with several other candidates. After sitting through a presentation, he learned that the product he would be selling was a line of health and wellness supplements. John was excited; he loved taking care of himself and working out, and he thought this self-employed position would be a great fit.

He watched as other presenters took to the stage, each one whipping the assembled audience into a frenzy. Here, at last, was the golden opportunity John had been looking for. He listened intently as the presenters boasted about the substantial earnings that could be made, how they had found freedom, and how the company had rewarded them with luxury cruises and other fantastic perks. By the end of the presentation, John couldn't wait to sign up for this fantastic opportunity.

There was a fee for joining, but in return, John would be able to sign others up. He also received a distributor's kit, which included a couple of sample products and a training manual. John was surprised when the person who signed him up suggested that he buy a selection of other products, not only to show potential customers but to "prove how serious he was about the opportunity"

John was shocked by just how expensive the company's products were, but he swallowed hard and handed over his credit card to pay the bill of several hundred dollars. After all, the presenters had assured the audience that these products were fantastic, so they would practically sell themselves. And after all, he had just had his redundancy payment.

John took the products home, eager to show his wife his new business and the products that would improve their lives. He was surprised by how little enthusiasm his wife showed for his haul. She said that she had seen similar products advertised far more cheaply than the ones John had just purchased, and she didn't think the business would work. In fact, she even asked John if he could get his money back.

Unperturbed by his wife's lack of interest, John read the sales manual from cover to cover and then called his friends individually. He felt sure they would support him in his new business venture; they were his closest allies. But John was shocked when he was met with a polite rebuff or an abrupt end to the call. Everyone said they were "too busy" or "didn't need any supplements.

However, John wasn't deterred by this lack of interest. After all, this was the latest big thing, and it was clear that his friends just weren't as visionary as he was. He clogged up his social media and those of his friends with information on the products. He even went door-to-door in his neighbourhood and took out advertisements in his local press. This last endeavour earned him an abrupt call from the company's head office, warning him that independent distributors were not allowed to advertise the company's products in the media.

John put his entire heart and soul into the business, but no matter what he did, he couldn't make it work. He knew he could sell; he had been good at it before, so why wasn't anyone interested in the products?

In desperation, John turned to his upline and his upline's upline for help. But they weren't really interested in giving John any sound advice. Instead, they encouraged him to buy even more products so they could reach their targets

Eventually, John quit the business. Disillusioned and thousands of dollars out of pocket, he swore never to get involved in sales again.

So, what did John and Mary do wrong? Absolutely nothing. They put all their efforts into their businesses but couldn't make them work. This outcome is by far the most common with MLM. People go into it with great enthusiasm. They do everything they can to build up their business but ultimately fail.

But failing in an MLM environment isn't personal. There are many factors at play here that are beyond the control of individual distributors. There may just not be a market for what you are selling, or that market may be oversaturated. Products might be overpriced. Many people have a general dislike of MLMs and will avoid them whenever possible.

All too often, though, upline and even the MLM company are quick to pass the blame onto the distributor for the failure of their business. "*You just didn't try hard enough*", "*you just didn't believe in the product enough*" or "*you didn't really want to be successful*" are just some of the blame tactics your upline might use to disguise the fact that the company offers an unsustainable business model.

Worse still, the cult-like behaviour might kick in, and you might find yourself excluded or treated like a pariah. Some distributors are encouraged to refrain from contacting or interacting with anyone who has left the business. This fear of being socially punished or excluded is actually a powerful way to stop people from leaving the company.

I have heard and seen examples of people being told they can no longer be friends with anyone who has left the company. Sometimes, these individuals are even told they cannot associate with their family members. The grip of MLM can be incredibly strong, and stopping your friends and family from having contact with you is one of the most hurtful and damaging forms of control.

If you feel that you have somehow failed because you could not make a success of MLM, don't think that way. It's not you; it's them. You may have felt excited and elated when you started your business, only to find that your journey has entered a path of disappointment and debt.

MLM companies sell dreams to people based on the idea of freedom and financial independence. However, for most people, it will remain just that, a dream.

If you realise that MLM is not for you, cut your losses and find a more sustainable and realistic way to start your own business. Seek advice from trusted business advisors, or consider starting small with a side hustle. Don't be fooled by the myth that investing more time and money into your MLM business will turn things around. It probably won't.

Sarah's Story

Sarah was recruited by her friend Cathy into an MLM. Although Sarah enjoyed the excitement of running her own business, she was starting to become frustrated as sales were slow. She invested more money into the business, but was not breaking even. Most months, she lost a lot more money than she was making.

Cathy, the upline responsible for Sarah's recruitment, showed no sympathy or support for Sarah's financial plight. She simply advised Sarah to continue advertising and investing additional money in the business. Sarah was stuck in an impossible situation. After much consideration, Sarah decided she had to cut her losses.

However, all was not in vain. Sarah had had a taste of what it would be like to run her own business, and she was determined to work for herself. She spent all her spare time researching her options and eventually started her own business selling hair extensions and makeup

Sarah sourced her products from ethical suppliers, and her USP (unique selling point) was that everything she sold was vegan and cruelty-free. She also created a YouTube channel where she posted tutorial videos, which not only provided helpful hints and tips on beauty but also demonstrated how to use her products. Her tutorials on applying hair extensions won her a new audience.

Sarah used her MLM experience as a springboard to greater and higher things. She can run her business how she wants and has just taken on her first employee.

ARE THERE ANY REAL BENEFITS TO MLM?

There are a few, in fact, very few, people making a great living at MLM. These individuals account for a fraction of one per cent of everyone who has ever been involved in MLM. On the surface, they appear to have enviable lifestyles. These are the stars that MLM companies love to showcase as shining examples, demonstrating that anyone can achieve a fantastic lifestyle if they work hard enough.

I have met some of the very top distributors in MLM schemes, and they are far from ordinary. They tend to have massive self-belief, drive and a wide circle of influence. In short, they would probably rise to the top of most professions they tried. Additionally, they managed to capitalise on opportunities at the beginning and build large teams. They had the benefit of a relatively new product on the market. Is it possible for an average person with average connections to achieve this level of success? Technically, yes, but it is very unlikely.

I have also observed that when an MLM company closes, its top distributors often become very successful in other MLM companies. Because they have readymade networks of contacts, they will just recruit these into the new opportunity and start over. They are good at persuading people to join a new network; they will always have a certain advantage that helps them rise to the top.

While few people make a living at MLM, there are other benefits to getting involved. The greatest of these is in personal development and networking. You get to meet others with an entrepreneurial mindset, and whilst MLM has damaged friendships, it has also forged them.

There is usually a significant personal development element involved in MLM, which can be both interesting and useful in other aspects of life. Skills such as improving communication, leadership, and the fundamentals of sales and marketing can be applied to both your personal and professional life.

MLM meetings are often held in high-quality hotels and banqueting suites, with no expense spared. While distributors may have to pay to attend some of these events, the company typically covers the costs for the most part. So, if you enjoy touring function rooms and visiting nice hotels, then MLM is a great fit for you. And of course, don't forget the trips that you have to pay to go on!!!

MLM lets you dip your toes into the business world at a very low cost. As long as you aren't tempted to make a massive investment in stocks, it can be a side hustle that lets you learn about marketing and selling products without the expense of setting up a traditional business. Be aware that your friends and family might buy from you once as a goodwill gesture, but they are unlikely to become long-term customers. Avoid alienating them with a hard sell!

MLM MINEFIELD

Marketing MLM products can be an absolute minefield, and people have found themselves on the wrong side of the law for making claims about products which cannot be backed up with evidence. It is easy to get carried away when promoting your business and end up on the wrong side of consumer law.

The following guidance is based on advice from the Advertising Standards Authority in the UK and applies to distributors and companies that operate in the UK. There may be different rules in other parts of the world. Most reputable MLMs provide guidance on what is and is not acceptable when promoting products and will take action against anyone who flouts the rules.

It is your job as a distributor and the company's responsibility to ensure that any advertising, claims or statements about a product are accurate, fair and backed up by evidence. You must not mislead potential buyers, even unintentionally.

You must always provide clear and accurate information about the products or services you are selling. Don't make claims that are exaggerated, unproven or unsupported.

You must not make any income guarantees or claims about the income potential of the business.

Ensure you are aware of and comply with any legal requirements associated with the MLM business.

Don't make false or misleading claims about your products to your potential customers.

Always be as open and transparent as possible when promoting your business and your products. Make it clear that you are an independent distributor of [insert company name] and do not work directly for the company. Avoid making any claims that imply you are authorised to act on behalf of the company in any capacity other than as an independent self-employed distributor.

 While you might be eager to recruit others for the opportunity, avoid using underhanded tactics to encourage people to contact you. It is particularly deceitful to advertise an MLM opportunity as a part-time job on a job board unless you make it extremely clear that this is a self-employed opportunity without a guarantee of income.

There are certain categories of products for which additional requirements apply. These include weight loss or weight control products, anti-ageing and skincare products, food supplements and pills, aromatherapy items, CBD oil, products containing alcohol, e-cigarettes and vaping products, and hair-care items.

LIABILITY

You can be held liable for any unsubstantiated claims you make about products, even if those claims were actually provided to you by the brand. Any claims you make, especially concerning health or weight loss products, must be backed up by watertight evidence, including clinical trials.

Both customers and MLM companies can sue individual distributors within the MLM companies. If you make untrue claims about a product, cause the company to come into disrepute or damage the brand in any way. Some companies have very strict policies regarding advertising and the use of acceptable wording. It might be OK to say, "I love the taste of this product", but you cannot say, "This is the tastiest product on the market."

Many MLM companies have found themselves in hot water with advertising and trade regulators and, in some cases, have been forced to stop trading. Naturally, they will do everything they can to protect their name and image, even if that does mean throwing the occasional distributor under the bus.

One MLM company filed a lawsuit against a woman who started a Facebook group, alleging that the company's products were causing damage to people. In return, several people who believed the company's products had caused them harm filed class-action lawsuits.

Claims that the product can help with any health condition are strictly prohibited. Only a licensed medical practitioner can make health claims, and even then, under strict circumstances. Genuine, correctly formulated medical trials must support health claims, and the evidence for any claims must be watertight.

If a consumer sees a claim about a product that is untrue, they may have grounds for a lawsuit. Even worse, if the product has caused the consumer harm, they may be able to sue for a substantial amount. Don't assume that your MLM agreement will indemnify you against claims of this kind. If a consumer decides to come after you, you could be in hot water.

FALSE IMPRESSIONS

Promoting products with false impressions, such as filtering or airbrushing models to make the product appear better, is classed as false advertising and can get you sued and terminated from an opportunity. Any promotional photography you use must not misleadingly exaggerate the benefits of a product, and any testimonials you use must be genuine. You must be able to provide the contact details of the person endorsing the product.

Even applying a filter to a photograph of yourself on social media can fall under these regulations if it exaggerates the results of a product you are promoting. If you are selling false eyelashes and the filter makes them appear longer than they actually are, this could leave you open to claims of false advertising or misrepresentation.

BEST SELLING CLAIMS

Making claims that you have the number one product on the market or that your product is a best-seller can be a minefield. Unless you have concrete proof that your product has outsold every other competing product in its category, it is advisable not to make the claim. If you do have evidence, it should be included in the advert.

Remember, any copy you write must be honest, verifiable and factual. Because advertising products is such a minefield and getting it wrong can land both you and the company in hot water, you might be limited to only being able to use company-supplied copy on any adverts. It isn't easy to make your ad stand out from the crowd when you can only use mass-produced content.

HOW TO AVOID THE HIGH-PRESSURE MLM SALES PITCH

Some MLM pitches are so outrageous that they would be laughable if people weren't being tricked into parting with their money. So much so that there is even a forum over on Reddit dedicated to the most shocking MLM pitches - there are some real horrors in there. Like the MLM distributor who faked a flat tyre so that people would stop and help her, she could pitch to them! Other people were pitching at homeless shelters - I kid you not.

When faced with an aggressive sales pitch, don't be pressured into doing something you don't want to. Never be afraid to say no, or I'm just not interested. If they continue to pester you, consider walking away or leaving the situation. Your time and personal space are precious, and no one has the right to invade them.

Things might get awkward, but this is not your fault. You might spot the signs of a potential MLM pitch before it happens. For example, if someone you haven't spoken to in a while suddenly messages out of the blue, there could be an impending "Hun moment" coming. Likewise, if someone invites you to an unexpected party or a meeting at a hotel, be aware that you might be in for a sales pitch.

We are all disposed to help a friend in need, but that does not give them the right to exploit us. If your friend gives you a sob story about no one buying their products, don't just give in to a sympathy buy, especially if you don't want the product. Commiserate with them and wish them good luck but avoid discussing why you don't want to buy.

MLM DAMAGES RELATIONSHIPS

MLM's damage to relationships and friendships can be considerable and lasting. When one partner is enthusiastic about MLM and the other is not, it can put a significant strain on the relationship.

Recruits are often told to cut ties with negative people, but when that person is your partner or spouse, this isn't going to happen. But MLM can cause real and permanent damage to a partnership, which might even end the relationship altogether.

The involved partner may see the other as unsupportive for refusing to get involved or dismissing their efforts. The non-involved partner may be annoyed by the constant promotion and marketing of MLM products, as well as the time the business consumes. If one partner uses shared funds to finance the business, this will naturally lead to resentment and rows.

Another sticking point is involving friends and family. It can cause embarrassment and anger if joint contacts are pressured into joining. Furthermore, friends and relations may feel obliged to purchase products they don't want or need, leading to feelings that they are being exploited.

This strain can lead to resentment, arguments, and even withdrawal from the relationship. MLM companies understand that a sceptical partner will undermine the efforts of the involved partner, so they make great efforts to bring them on board if they can.

Even if both partners are involved in MLM, it can lead to arguments and conflict. Disagreements over the level of involvement, financial commitment, or involving family and friends, as well as the amount of time and energy the business is consuming, are common.

Tony and Barbara were jointly involved in an MLM business, but Barbara felt that Tony was investing too much money and time into it. They rarely spent time together anymore and never went out as a couple unless it was related to their MLM activities. Barbara had initially been enthusiastic about the business but was now beginning to resent it.

On the other hand, Tony could not understand Barbara's change of heart. In his mind, they were building something that would benefit them both in the future. He didn't realise how much strain was being put on the relationship.

Friendships can be damaged in similar ways. Friends who constantly try to pitch to others will soon find that people are going out of their way to avoid them. When friends feel like they are being manipulated or pressured into buying or recruiting, it destroys the trust between them.

Becky was the person in her friendship group who always tried to sell something to her friends. It started with make-up but soon involved weight loss products, false nails, cookware, books, and baby products. Becky was always convinced she was onto the next big thing, but after a few weeks, she would change her mind and try something else.

At first, her friends were supportive. They bought Becky's products because they cared about her and wanted her to succeed. But after a while, they grew tired of being constantly pitched products whenever they met up with Becky. They started avoiding her and deliberately not inviting her to meet-ups because they knew she would only try to turn them into sales pitches.

We all know someone like Becky, and the chances are they are or have been involved in MLM! It's easy to get caught up in the enthusiasm of a new venture, but it can be equally damaging to friendships if it's not reined in.

The damage to relationships and friendships is rarely discussed in

MLM circles, but it is a genuine issue. But MLM has led to far more sinister outcomes. For one man, it led to the murder of his wife and attempted suicide.

MLM MURDER

Ellery Bennett from West Bloomfield, USA, first became involved in MLM in 2007. Lured by the idea of financial freedom, he was every inch the enthusiastic recruit, believing wholeheartedly in the company's promises. He knew that if he worked hard enough, he could be successful.

The company he had initially signed up for sold personal development products, including a flagship product —a 60-day course that cost over $1,000. Unfortunately, Ellery fell hook, line and sinker for the fake-it-until-you-make-it facade. On the surface, he was every inch the successful family man, but behind the scenes, Ellery faced a growing mountain of debt.

No one knew about Ellery's money troubles apart from his wife, Lisa. Eventually, she grew tired of the situation she found herself in, and on Aug 11, 2010, Lisa filed for divorce. A decision that would prove to be fatal.

One week later, on Wednesday, 18th August 2010, Ellery stabbed his wife, Lisa, to death. He then attempted suicide but presented at a local hospital to be treated.

In February 2011, Ellery Bennett was found guilty of the murder of his wife, Lisa Bennett. He was sentenced to life imprisonment without the possibility of parole.

Tragically, Lisa Bennett may be alive today if her husband had not gotten involved in MLM. Undoubtedly, a significant portion of Ellery Bennett's debt problems can be attributed directly to his MLM businesses.

Fortunately, not all outcomes are as tragic as this, but it does serve as a grim reminder of the pressure that MLM can place on relationships.

LEAVING AN MLM

If you are involved in an MLM and are starting to have cold feet, it's never too late to cut your losses and walk away. Don't wait until you're haemorrhaging money and up to your eyeballs in credit card debt before you make that call. Admitting that MLM isn't for you is a brave decision, but one you are unlikely to regret. Revisit the statistics at the beginning of the book or ask an impartial friend for their opinion. Then, once you have decided to leave, don't let others pressure you into changing your mind.

There is likely to be intense pressure on you not to leave, coming from your upline. Remember that the more members stay in the system, the more potential money they can make from you. Don't be taken in by their promises that you will succeed if you stick it out a little bit longer, because it is unlikely to be true. Realistically, things probably won't change for the better, but you might get poorer.

I have heard of every psychological trick in the book used to stop people from leaving MLM, in much the same way cults put huge efforts into preventing people from getting out. Your entire upline might be called upon "to change your mind" and place extreme pressure on you. Remember that there is a 50/50 chance that they won't even be involved in the opportunity in twelve months, so remain steadfast in your determination to leave.

REFUSE TO PLAY THE BLAME GAME

Don't blame yourself for not being able to make things work, and don't let anyone else try to shame you, either. Equally, leave professionally and avoid burning bridges that don't need to be burned. Avoid posting negative reviews of the products or business on social media. If anyone asks why you left, tell them it wasn't for you and leave it at that.

CHECK YOUR AGREEMENT

Before you decide to leave, review the fine print in your MLM distributor agreement to determine the official method for terminating the plan. If you don't officially quit, you may find yourself subject to an inactivity clause, but you will not be officially removed from the distributor list. This would subject you to the company's ongoing terms and conditions, without deriving any benefit from them.

If you are an MLM leader (yes, leaders quit, too) or have reached a certain level in the business, and you quit, you may be subject to different terms and conditions. You might be subject to non-solicitation or non-compete orders depending on your agreement with the company. This may mean that you cannot join a different MLM with similar products and cannot solicit your downline for any competing opportunity within a specified time frame. If you think this might be the case, ask a legal professional to look at your agreement to tell you precisely what you can and can't do.

UNSOLD PRODUCT

Most distributors who leave MLM will find themselves with at least some unsold products; for some, the value of these products may be substantial. Check if the company has a buy-back clause, and if so, what are the terms? The company will likely only accept new and unopened items, in date and original condition. Even if the company is willing to buy back the products, there is likely to be some form of penalty. A "restocking fee" is not uncommon, which the company will deduct from your unsold stock for the privilege of taking it back. Alternatively, they may offer a sum well below what you paid for it and require you to pay the shipping costs.

Returning the stock to the company might not be the most

profitable way to deal with unsold inventory. Your upline or downline may be interested in purchasing the products at a discount, so it might be worth offering them to them first. However, remember that purchasing from you will not count towards their volume requirement, if they have one, so you need to sweeten the deal.

It may surprise you that some MLM companies prohibit their products from being sold on online auction sites or marketplaces. Furthermore, online auction sites and marketplaces also prohibit the sale of such products. Occasionally, MLM products slip through the filters, but be prepared for a takedown notice and your product to be delisted if you attempt to sell in this manner. It is probably better to try to resell back to the company, even if you do take a hit on your outlay.

Finally, remember to cancel any recurring orders you have for products. It is surprising how many distributors overlook this step.

SAYING GOODBYE

Letting your upline and downline know that you are leaving is probably the most challenging part of the process. They will likely react negatively, either pressuring you to stay or reacting with anger and hurt. Some might even take it personally, almost as if you are ending a friendship. In that case, prepare yourself for a cold shoulder and rebrand yourself as someone who "used to be in MLM".

Contacting each person individually with a short message and wishing them well in the future is sufficient. Don't feel you have to explain yourself or justify your reason for leaving; this sets you up to be re-convinced to join if your objections can be quashed.

Remember that you are making a brave decision, not one out of weakness. You are taking back control of your life and financial future. Some people speak of the intense relief they experience when they finally decide to say goodbye to MLM. View the experience as a learning opportunity and move forward.

Lastly, tie up any outstanding financial matters related to the business. Ensure that your books are up to date and all records are complete. Your profits may be taxable, depending on your location. Some countries, such as the UK, have a trading allowance threshold below which you qualify for full relief on profits. Currently, in the UK, the threshold is set at £1000, so many MLM distributors would fall under it. However, always seek tax advice from an expert, rather than relying on a book on *MLM*.

EVALUATING AN MLM OPPORTUNITY

Here is a quick cheat sheet for evaluating MLM opportunities.

The Company
Who is the company?
How long have they been established?
What are people saying about them? What is their reputation like?
Who are the key players?
What main stories come up when you search for them online? Are there numerous reviews, and are they mostly positive or negative?

The Product
What are the products you will be selling?
Would you use them yourself?
Is it worth the asking price?
Is there a market for this product?
What competing products are there in the marketplace?
How much do these competing products sell for?
What is the USP of the product (unique selling point)?
Who are your customers?
Does the product lend itself to repeat sales?

Business Opportunity
What is the cost to get involved?
Will I need to purchase stock upfront?
Am I expected to make any additional outlay?

How many tiers are there in the commission system?
Is there a minimum volume requirement to stay active/earn commission?
What is the commission structure? Does it seem viable?
Is there an inactivity fee?
Is there a buy-back clause in the agreement for any unsold stock?
Do I need to maintain a minimum number of customers to stay active?
What is the procedure if I want to leave?

Logistics

How will I get the product to my customers? Does the company ship directly to customers, or do I have to ship it myself?
Does the company offer free shipping?
What is the returns process, and who is responsible for refunds?
How long does shipping take?
What is the average time for customers to receive their orders?

Marketing

Can I envision myself marketing the product(s) in a unique and appealing way?
How can I add value to this opportunity/product?
Are the products regulated products? For example, health, weight loss or beauty products?
Does the company provide advertising material?
What are the rules for selling products online?
Can I sell on social media?
Online auction sites?
Online marketplaces?
Am I allowed to place print adverts or flyers?

THE HIDDEN COSTS OF MLM

In addition to the initial costs of paying your registration fee and purchasing a starter kit, there are other expenses associated with MLM that many people overlook. These can not only swallow up any commissions you earn but can also be substantial. When costs are factored in, an opportunity that seemed lucrative may no longer be so attractive

COST OF BUYING PRODUCTS.

Whilst your starter kit may come with some products, most distributors will want to order at least some additional stock. Not only will you need products for personal use, but you will also need to be able to show them to others and quickly fulfil orders.

Depending on the business, even a small selection of products can add up. If you need to purchase a minimum number of products to stay active in the scheme, factor this into any calculations. How realistic is it that you will be able to find enough customers to avoid inactivity penalties, or will you be lumbered with unsold stock?

ADVERTISING AND MARKETING.

This includes the cost of running any social media sites, website and other online presence. Additionally, the cost of printed materials, such as flyers, posters, postcards, business cards, and any other promotional or recruitment materials.

Add to this any telephone or postage costs, and promoting your products can be quite pricey. This is one of MLM's most overlooked expenses and can often be a hefty one. Keep records of everything you spend promoting your MLM, and you might be surprised at how much outlay is involved.

SHIPPING

You must factor in shipping expenses if products aren't shipped directly from the MLM company to the customer. This can be exceptionally costly if you need to ship products internationally, especially if they are heavy or bulky.

Packaging items for shipment can be time-consuming and expensive, as you want to ensure they arrive at their destination safely and in good condition. Therefore, you will need to invest in various packaging boxes and materials, in addition to shipping charges.

TRAVEL

Most MLM companies hold at least monthly meetings for their distributors, which you are encouraged to attend. Since the pandemic, many of these have been held online as opposed to in person, but as we start to return to normal, they will likely resume face-to-face meetings. Additionally, there may be networking events, team get-togethers, and, of course, visits to potential customers.

Additionally, you may be invited to attend other events, such as MLM awards ceremonies, motivational courses, and miscellaneous events that occur throughout the year. These may also require additional expenditures on formal attire, meals, and drinks. If you need to stay overnight, factor in travel and hotel costs too.

Note down any mileage you incur while running your business, as well as any fares, tickets, or hotel stays you pay for. For some people, just the costs of attending regular meetings will outweigh the money they make from the business.

HOME OFFICE & RECORD KEEPING

Keeping yourself organised is a crucial aspect of running any business. For this reason, you might want to set up a home office. Whilst technically, the corner of a dining room table could serve as an office, most people like to create a separate space for working. This might involve an outlay on office furniture, at the very least, a desk and chair. Then you will need to find somewhere to keep your inventory and marketing material. Lastly, you need somewhere quiet to make business calls or hold online meetings.

Keeping accurate records of your income and expenses is a legal requirement for any business, regardless of its size. This includes recording any income you earn and any expenses you incur. You don't have to invest in expensive spreadsheets or accounting programs unless your business warrants it. However, you will probably also want to keep your paperwork organised so you can review it and refer to it when necessary. Investing in a good filing cabinet and a selection of folders and labels can help save time and keep your business up to date.

Being self-employed might require you to file additional tax returns, and if you have income and expense streams coming in from various sources, tax can be very complicated. In this case, you might need the services of an accountant at additional expense.

MISCELLANEOUS EXPENSES

Depending on what you are selling and how you are selling it, you may encounter additional costs beyond those we have already mentioned. These could include renting a stall in a craft fair or market, displaying materials for your products, product samples to hand out and training costs.

Some MLM companies emphasise personal development, and although not compulsory, you may invest in additional materials, such as books and digital downloads. Even networking, which is at the heart of all MLM, doesn't come for free; you usually have to travel to a venue and when there, you will probably pay for some form of refreshments.

It is easy to invest a significant amount of money in an MLM business beyond the initial start-up costs. Consider the cost of doing business when evaluating an opportunity.

CONCLUSION

I hope this book has provided you with some insight into the world of MLM and has saved you time and money. If you still wish to proceed after reading this, I genuinely wish you all the best. However, if this book has stopped you in your tracks and made you think, and potentially helped you realise that MLM is not all it's cracked up to be for the vast majority of participants, I would be grateful if you would leave a review. Additionally, please share this book with anyone you think may find it useful. Perhaps even buy a copy for a friend who might be considering joining an MLM business.

And if you have tried and failed, it really isn't your fault. The system is against you, as you have learned over the last few chapters. Don't let this failure stop you from pushing ahead with a different type of business or let it dampen your entrepreneurial spirit. I wish you the very best.

MLM GLOSSARY

Compensation Plan – This is the document which outlines how much money you can make in the MLM, typically with a structure of commissions, overrides, residuals, bonuses and rewards.

Customer Volume – The total volume of sales to the customer

Direct Selling – A form of selling in which products are sold directly to the customer, typically in their own home, one-on-one, or at a party

Downline – This is the term used to describe your team of distributors and customers

MLM – Multi-Level Marketing – A business model which involves recruiting members to join you and selling products or services to customers

Organisation Volume – The total collective volume of sales of all members of the ML

Overrides – Additional commissions which you are eligible to earn from the sales of distributors in your downline

Qualifying Volume – The minimum amount of volume which must be achieved to stay active and continue to earn commission

Residuals – Commissions which you make from the sales of distributors in your downline

Retail Profit – The difference between the wholesale price and the recommended retail price

Retail Sales – Sales to customer

Upline – This is the term used to describe the person who recruited you into the MLM business

Wholesale Price – The price paid by a distributor to the MLM company for the product or service...

---

[i] https://www.ftc.gov/sites/default/files/documents/public_comments/trade-regulation-rule-disclosure-requirements-and-prohibitions-concerning-business-opportunities-ftc.r511993-00008%C2%A0/00008-57281.pdf

[ii] Berkowitz, Bill (January 28, 2009). "Republican Benefactor Launches Comeback". *Inter press service*. Retrieved September 19, 2018. (In reference to BERR vs Amway (Case No:2651, 2652 and 2653 of 2007) in point of objectionability's")

[iii] O'Donnell, Jayne (February 10, 2011). "Multilevel marketing or 'pyramid?' Salespeople find it hard to earn much". *USA Today*. Retrieved September 19, 2018.

[iv] Del Valle, Gaby (October 15, 2018). "Multilevel marketing companies say they can make you rich. Here's how much 7 sellers actually earned". *Vox*. Retrieved October 15, 2018.

[v] Singletary, Michelle. "Why multilevel marketing won't make you rich". *The Washington Post*. Retrieved October 22, 2018.

[vi] https://pinktruth.com/wp-content/uploads/taylor-mlm-study.pdf